Bear-ly Bear-able Baseball

RIDDLES, JOKES, AND KNOCK-KNOCKS

Written and illustrated by
MORT GERBERG

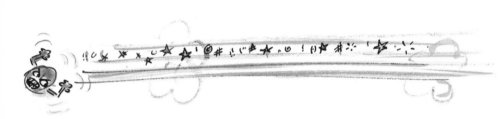

Featuring Riddle Bear

SCHOLASTIC INC.

New York Toronto London Auckland Sydney

For cousin Aaron

Other Scholastic books written and illustrated by Mort Gerberg

BEAR-LY BEAR-ABLE
Bear Riddles, Jokes, and Knock-Knocks

COMPUTER HOOTERS!
Computer Riddles, Jokes, and Knock-Knocks

WHY DID HALLEY'S COMET CROSS THE UNIVERSE?
And Other Riddles, Jokes, and Knock-Knocks

ISBN 0-590-42583-8

12 11 10 9 8 7 6 5 4 3 2 1   9/8 0 1 2 3 4/9

Printed in the U.S.A.   23

First Scholastic printing, September 1989

ROOTIN' TOON

Why would Kermit the Frog be a good outfielder?

Because frogs are excellent at catching flies.

Where do baseball players take their bats to clean them?

To the bat-room.

What did the baseball player's baby shout when he saw his father walk to home plate with a bat?

POP UP!

What would you call it if a pig hit a baseball over the fence, ran all around the bases, and stepped on home plate?

A ham run.

Why did Riddle Bear come up to home plate carrying a broom, a mop, a dustcloth, and a scrubbing brush?

He was the cleanup batter.

What kind of animal do you usually have at a baseball game?

A hot dog.

Riddle Bear wasn't wearing his sunglasses. However, he was *not* afraid that the sun would get in his eyes and make him drop the fly ball. Why?

He was playing a night game.

Knock. Knock.
Who's there?
Batter.
Batter who?
**Batter get a hit,
or we'll lose the game.**

Knock. Knock.
Who's there?
Pitcher.
Pitcher who?
**Pitcher sneakers on
if you want to play.**

Knock. Knock.
Who's there?
Ball four.
Ball four who?
Ball four you, glove for me.

Knock. Knock.
Who's there?
Defense.
Defense who?
**Defense is too far away
to hit de ball over.**

DID YOU EVER SEE . . .

A batter receiving a base on balls?

A player sliding into second base?

A batter getting a big hand after hitting a home run?

A catcher putting a tag on a sliding runner?

N THIS BASEBALL GAME?

CUBS	1/4	0	3/8	0	0	9/10					
BEARS	0	1/2	1/4	1 1/2	1/8						

4 FT

3476 FT

ONE WAY →

What would you call a baseball bat that you could also wear on your head?

A hat bat.

What would you call a pitch that makes you scratch yourself when it flies past?

An itchy pitch.

What would you call a baseball pitcher who makes more money than any other?

A richer pitcher.

PITCHER AND BATTER FUNNIES

A pitcher in the bullpen.

A pitcher warming up.

The batter holding his bat.

The batter ducking a wild pitch.

The batter at home plate.

The pitcher walking the batter.

AND DID YOU EVER SEE . . .

A home run?

A batter's box?

A pop fly?

A swinging batter?

What did the baseball shout when Superman hit it?
OUCH!

Why is being a good pitcher like making pancakes?
You have to really mix up the batter.

What has six arms and six legs and catches flies?

A baseball team's outfield.

Why did the gang of robbers sneak into the baseball stadium in the middle of the night?

They planned to steal the big diamond that was there

When is a base runner like an electric light?

When they're both out.

Why is an alarm clock different from a pitcher?

You have to wind up an alarm clock,
but a pitcher winds up by himself.

Why did the policeman run out on the field and arrest the ballplayer?

Because the player had just stolen second base.